I0797279

Words that are tricky to understand are in **bold**. Find out what they mean in the glossary.

Words that are difficult to say are in *italics*. Find out how to say them at the back of the book.

COULD THE HUMAN BRAIN POWER A LIGHT BULB?

DISCOVER THE SCIENCE BEHIND **NEUROBIOLOGY**
(ny-ugh-row-by-OH-luh-jee)

Written by Olivia Watson
Illustrated by Verónika Cháves Morales

WHAT IS NEUROBIOLOGY?

Neurobiology is the scientific study of the **nervous system**, including how it helps your body think, move, feel, and react to things.

The scientists who study neurobiology are called **NEUROBIOLOGISTS.**

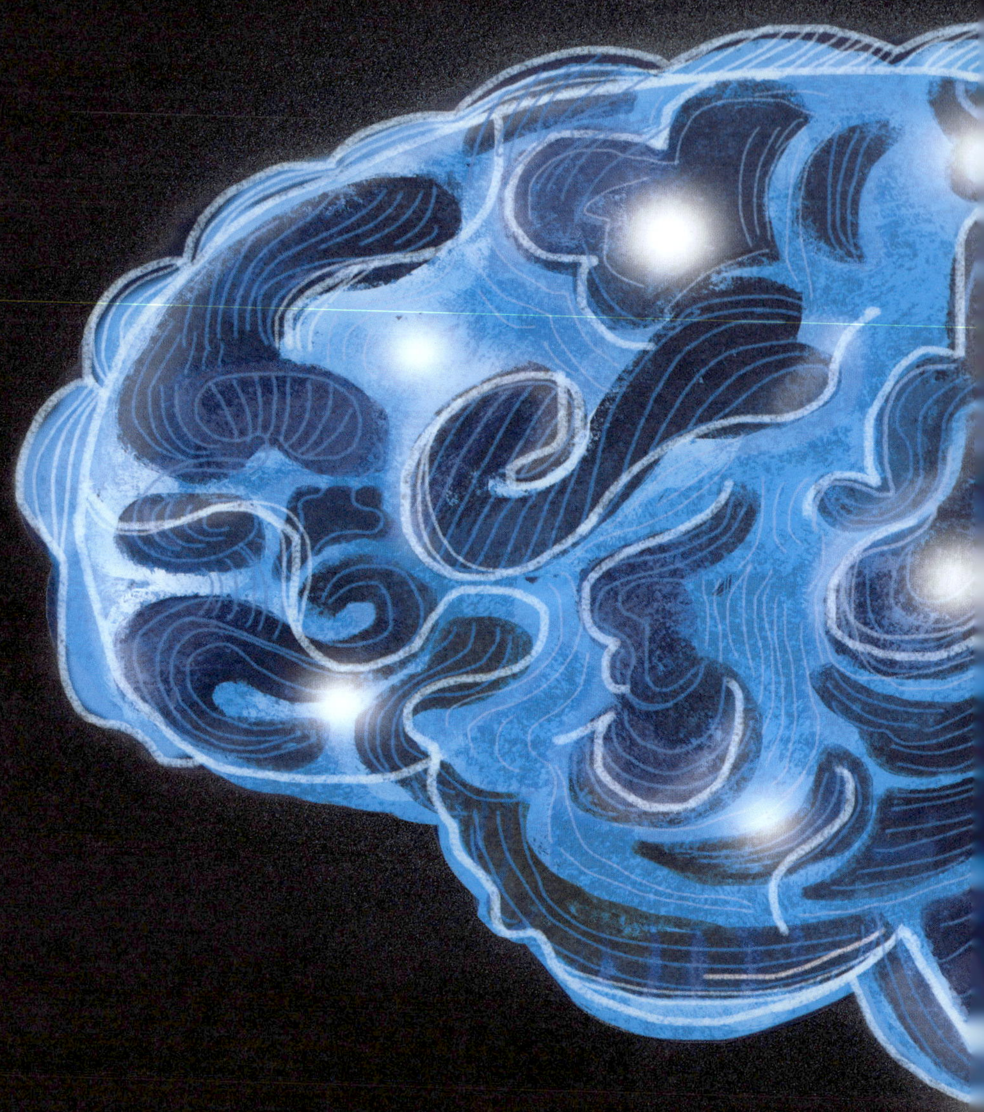

Your brain controls everything you do. From how you move, to how you think, learn, and feel, and the things you see, smell, and taste – it's all thanks to your brain.

Talented *neurobiologists* have taught us so much about this powerful **organ** in our heads, and are often learning more about its abilities…

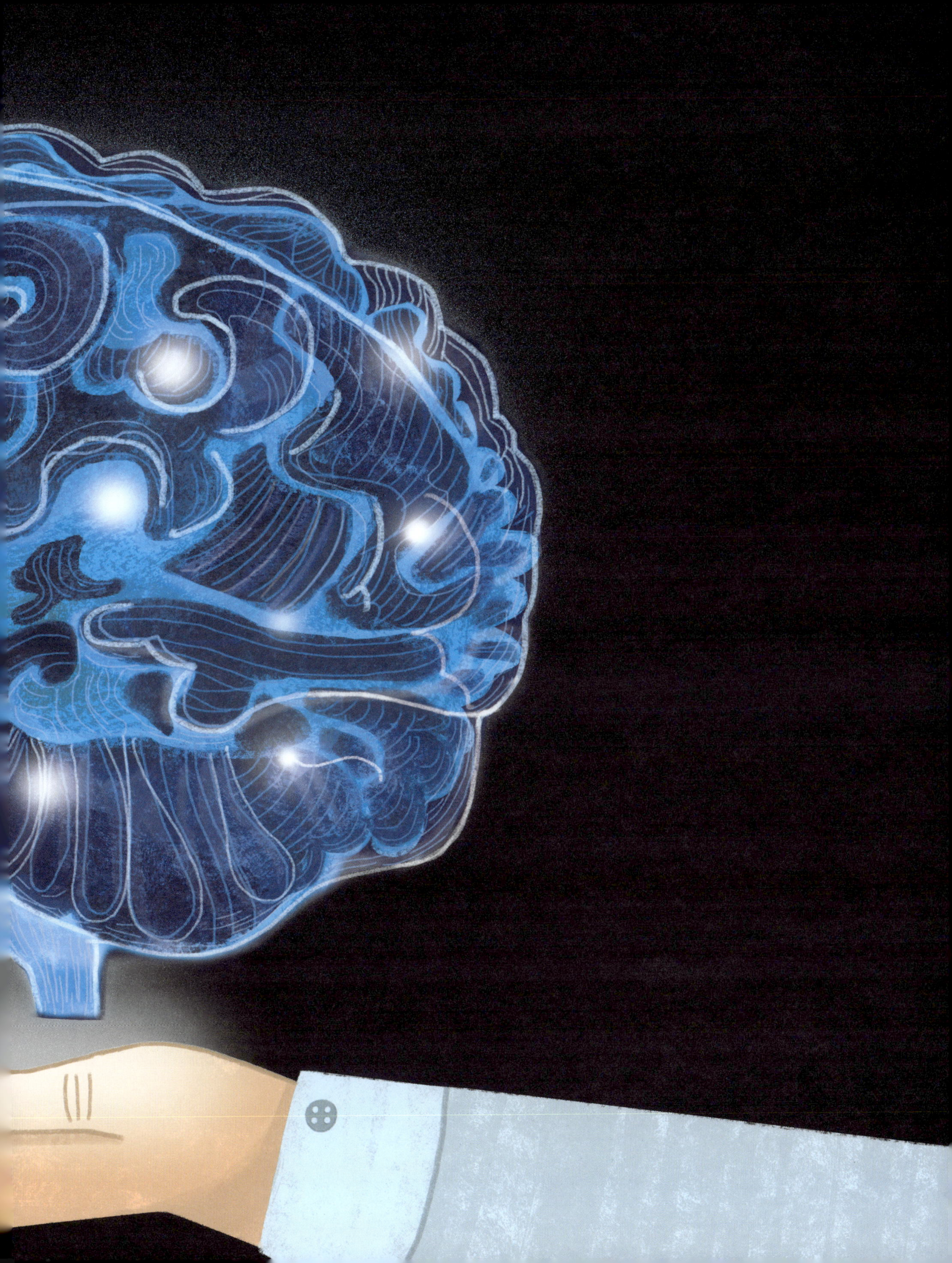

We didn't always know a lot about the brain. Thanks to old medical records, we know that long ago people like the ancient Egyptians believed the heart controlled people's thoughts and feelings.

It wasn't until the ancient Greeks studied the brain, many years later, that people began to understand the brain is really in charge of the body. But it took even longer for scientists to prove it!

But what actually is the brain? It's a squishy, wet lump of **tissue** inside our heads. Every human brain floats in a liquid inside the **skull** and connects to the **spine**. Most animals have a brain, but they don't all look or work the same. It's one reason animals can't talk, but humans can. So, how does it work?

The invention of the **microscope** and clever experiments helped neurobiologists understand just how complex the human brain is. Rather than being one lumpy mass, it's actually made of separate **nerve cells** which connect together like tree roots in a forest.

The human brain contains around 86 billion **neurons.** That's about the same as the number of stars in the

Milky Way galaxy!

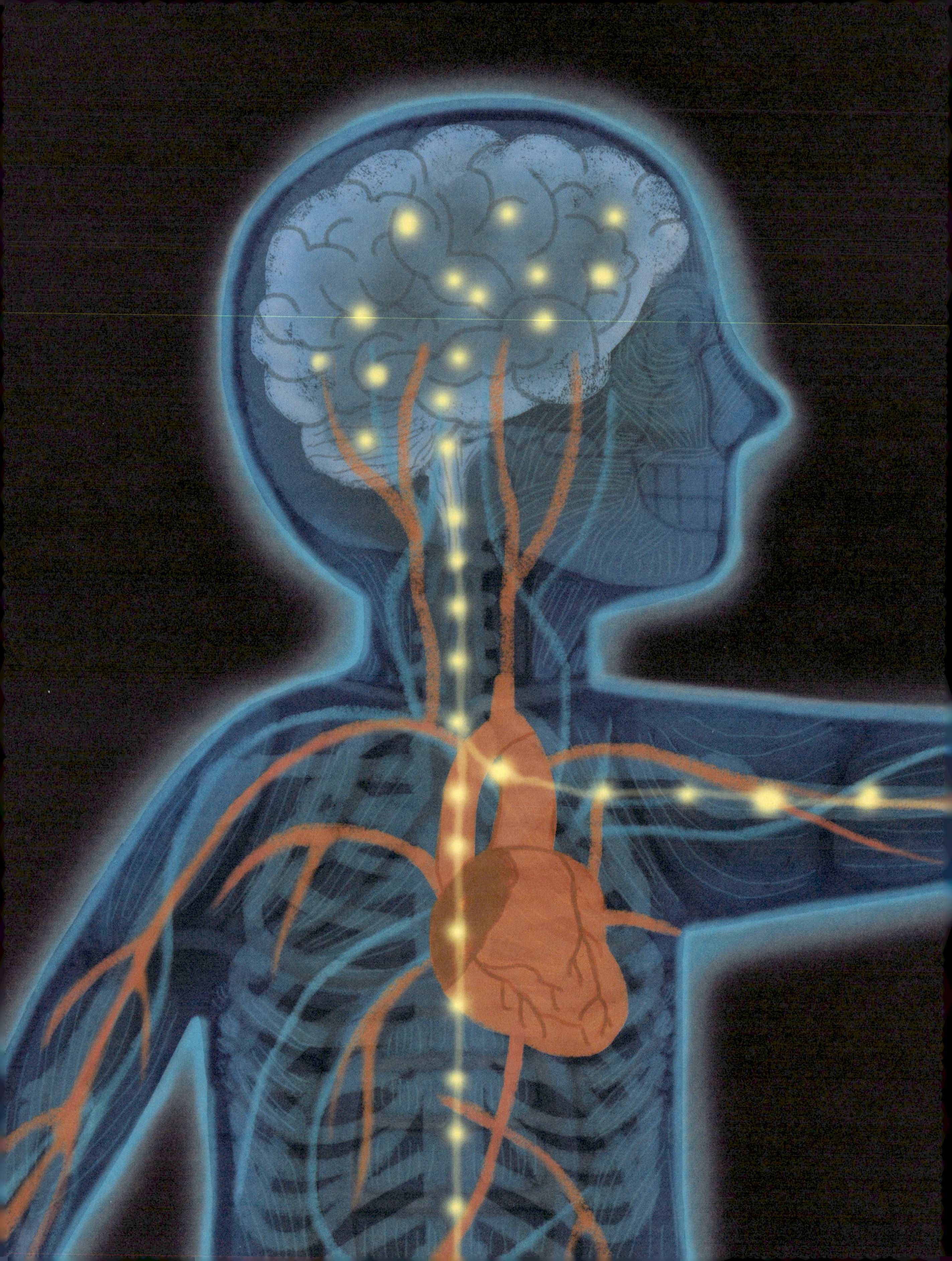

Scientists soon learned that nerve cells send messages between each other **using electricity!**

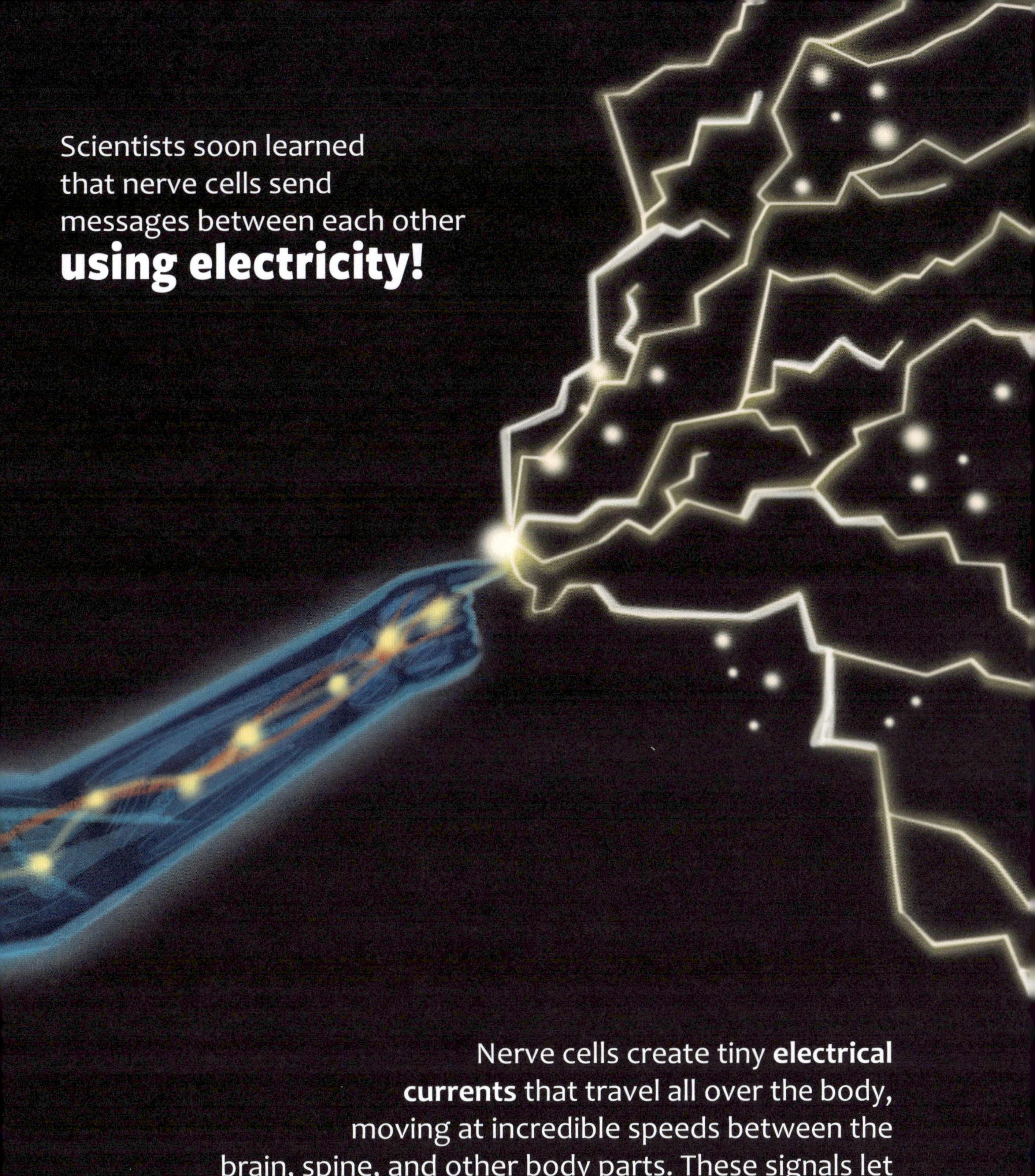

Nerve cells create tiny **electrical currents** that travel all over the body, moving at incredible speeds between the brain, spine, and other body parts. These signals let us do everything from walking to eating and thinking.

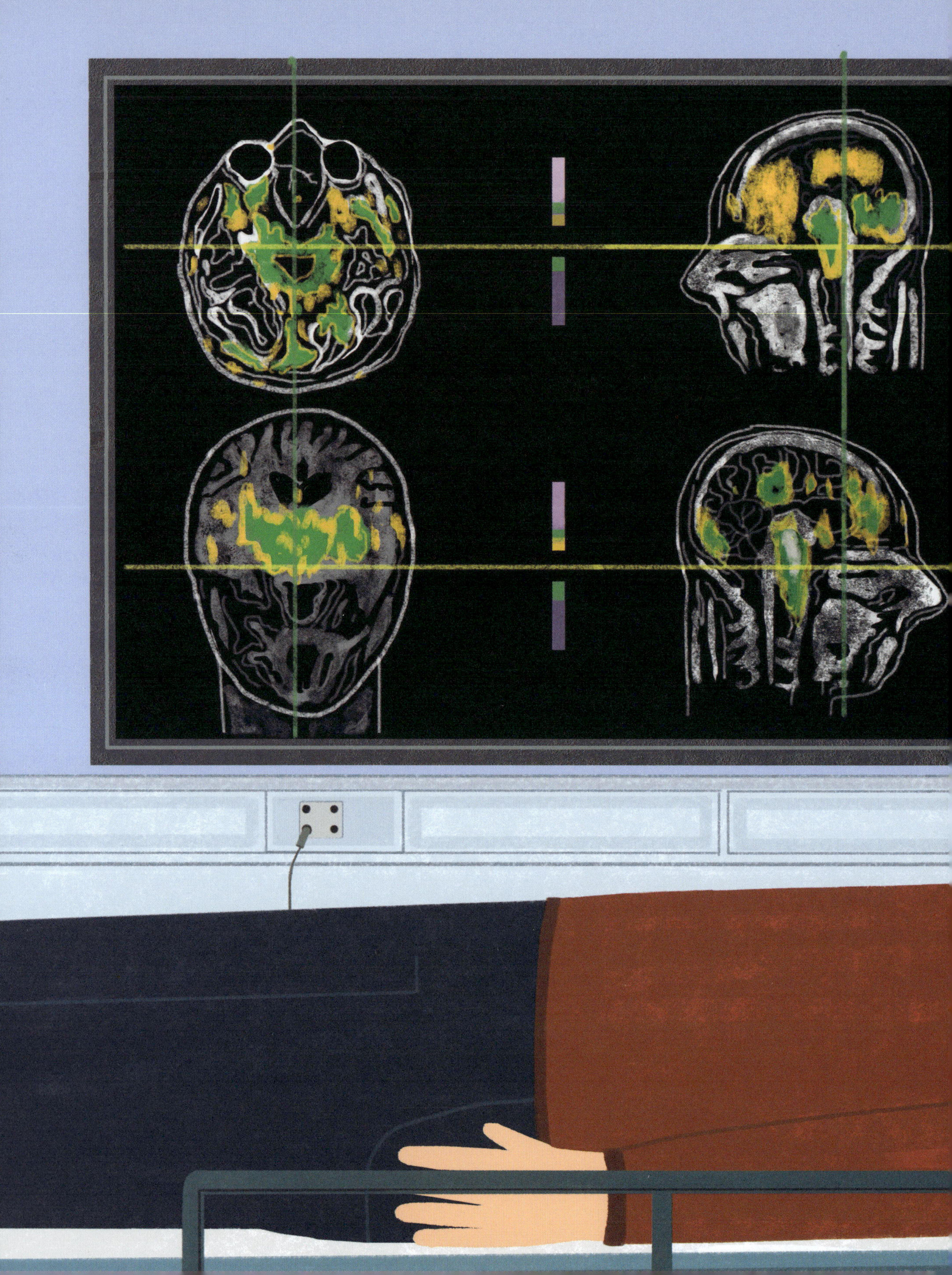

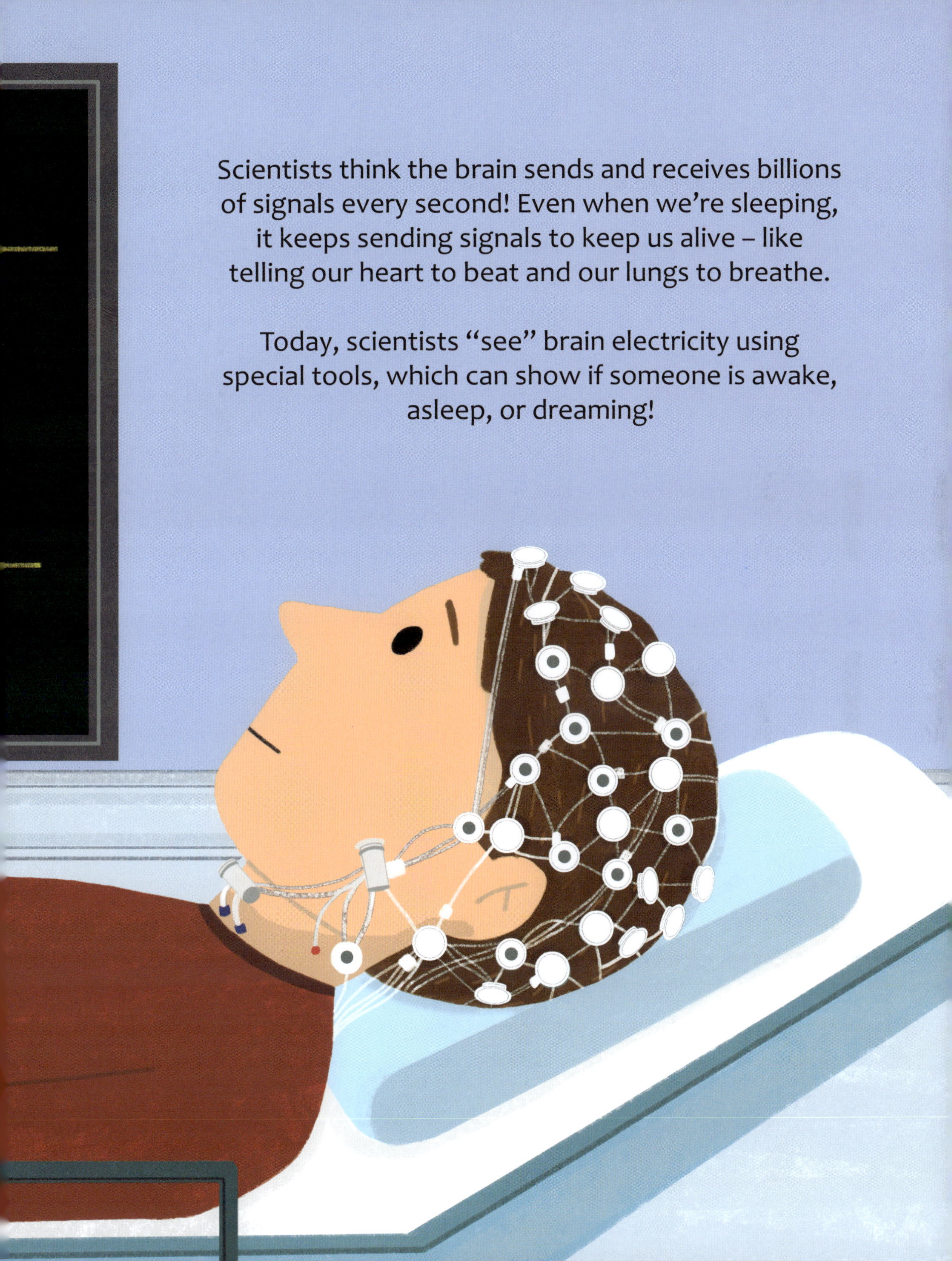

Scientists think the brain sends and receives billions of signals every second! Even when we're sleeping, it keeps sending signals to keep us alive – like telling our heart to beat and our lungs to breathe.

Today, scientists "see" brain electricity using special tools, which can show if someone is awake, asleep, or dreaming!

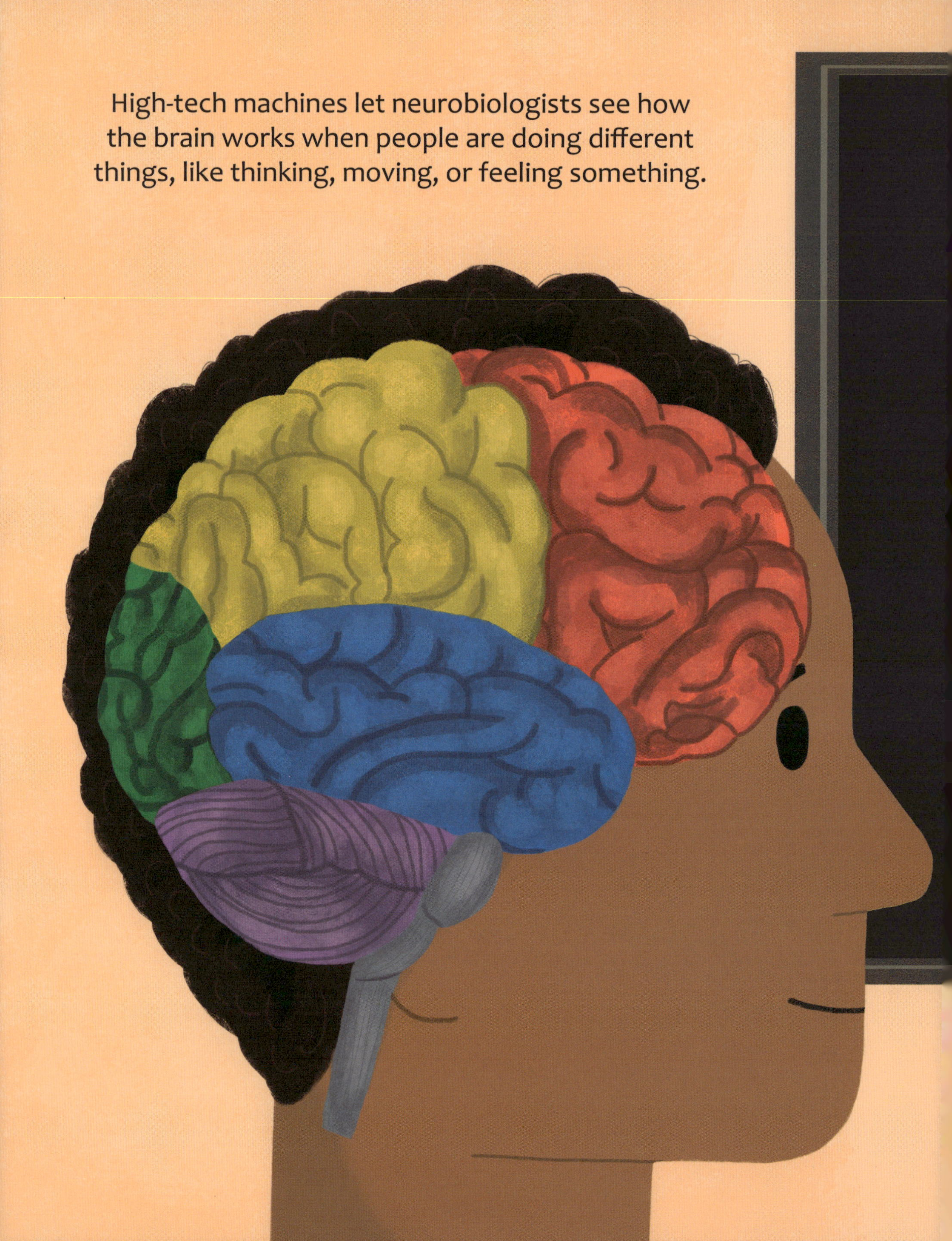

High-tech machines let neurobiologists see how the brain works when people are doing different things, like thinking, moving, or feeling something.

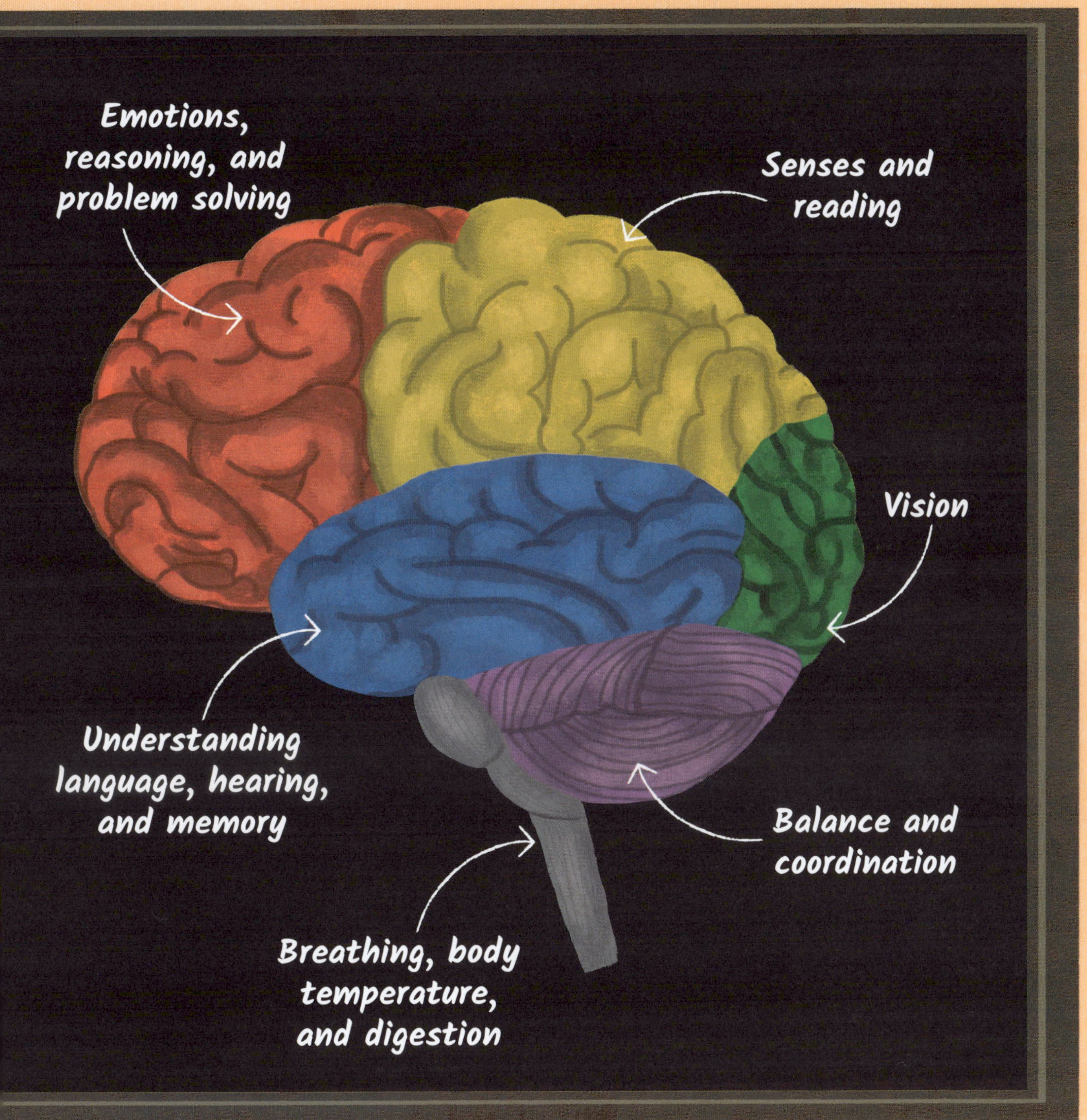

They've discovered that different parts of the brain control different things. This is helping them create detailed maps of the brain.

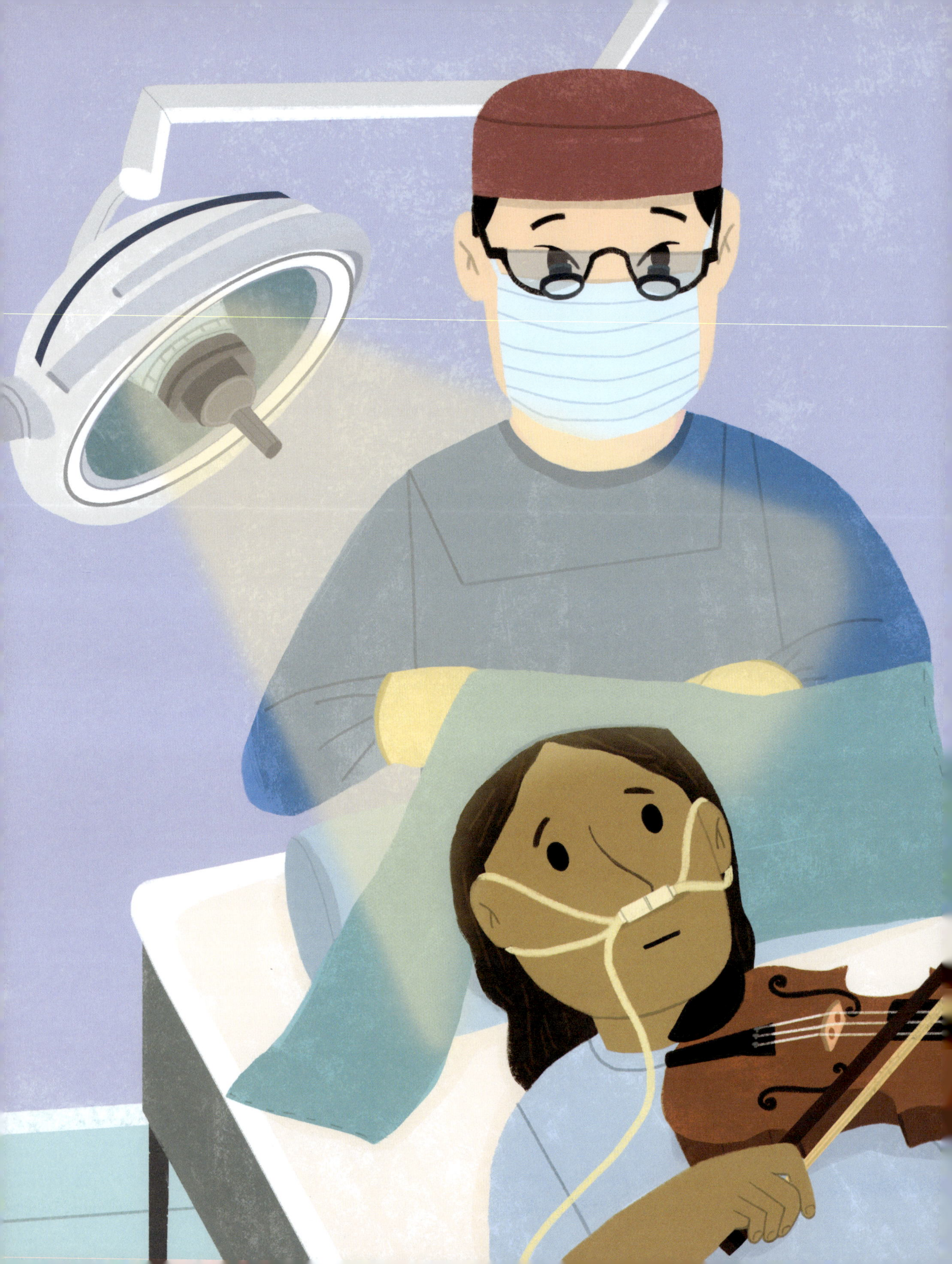

The brain can become damaged due to injury, **disease**, or old age, causing people to lose certain abilities, like memory. Knowing which part of the brain controls those abilities helps doctors treat damage and improve people's lives.

In some cases, talented doctors perform surgery on the brain which is done while the person is awake! Amazingly, brain tissue **feels no pain!**

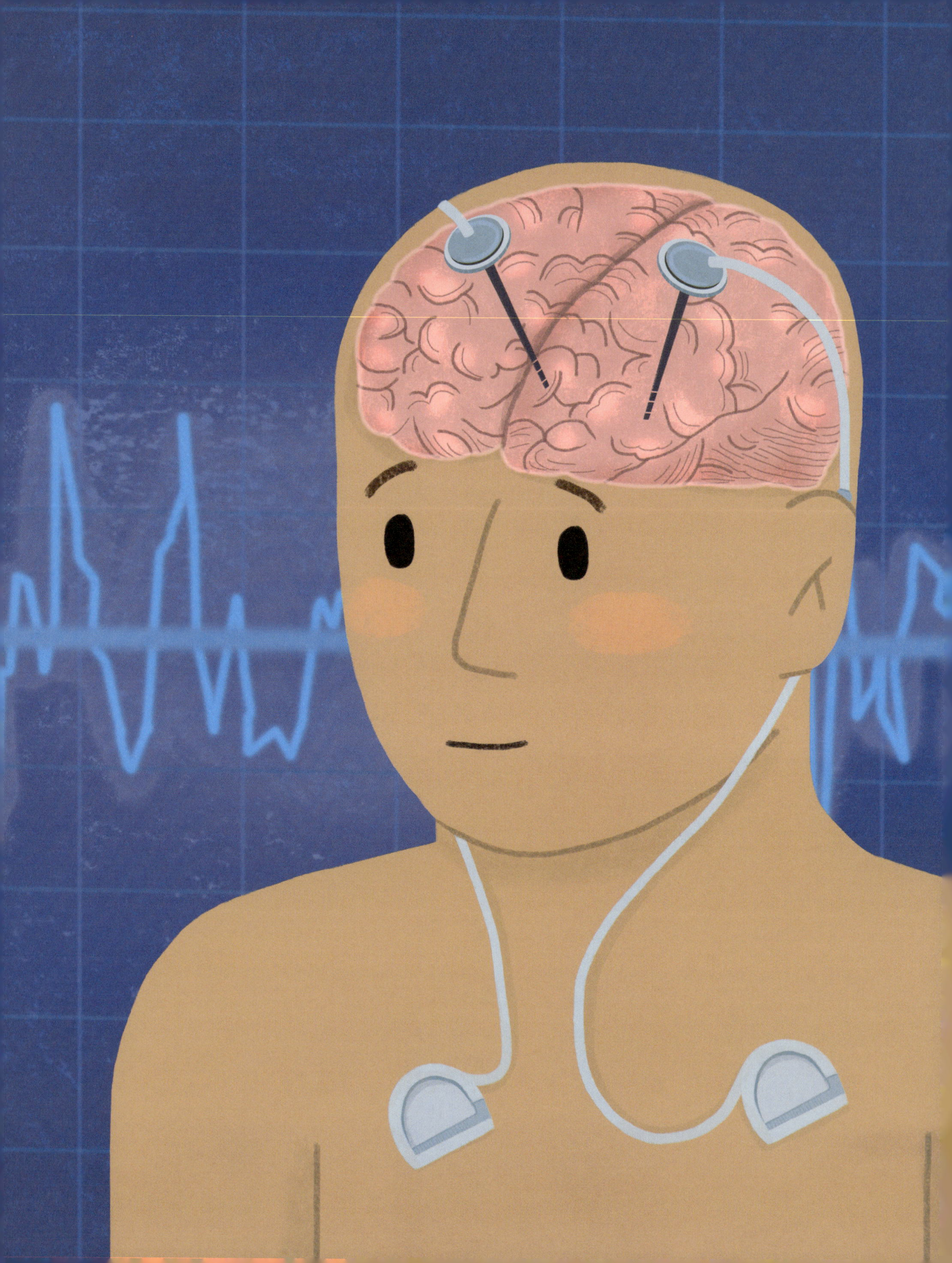

Sometimes surgery isn't possible. So neurobiologists are teaming up with engineers to create amazing technology instead.

They've designed tiny wires that send electrical signals like real nerve cells. Implanted in the brain, these wires monitor brain waves and help treat conditions like **Parkinson's**. In the future, **artificial** neurons shaped like computer chips might do similar jobs!

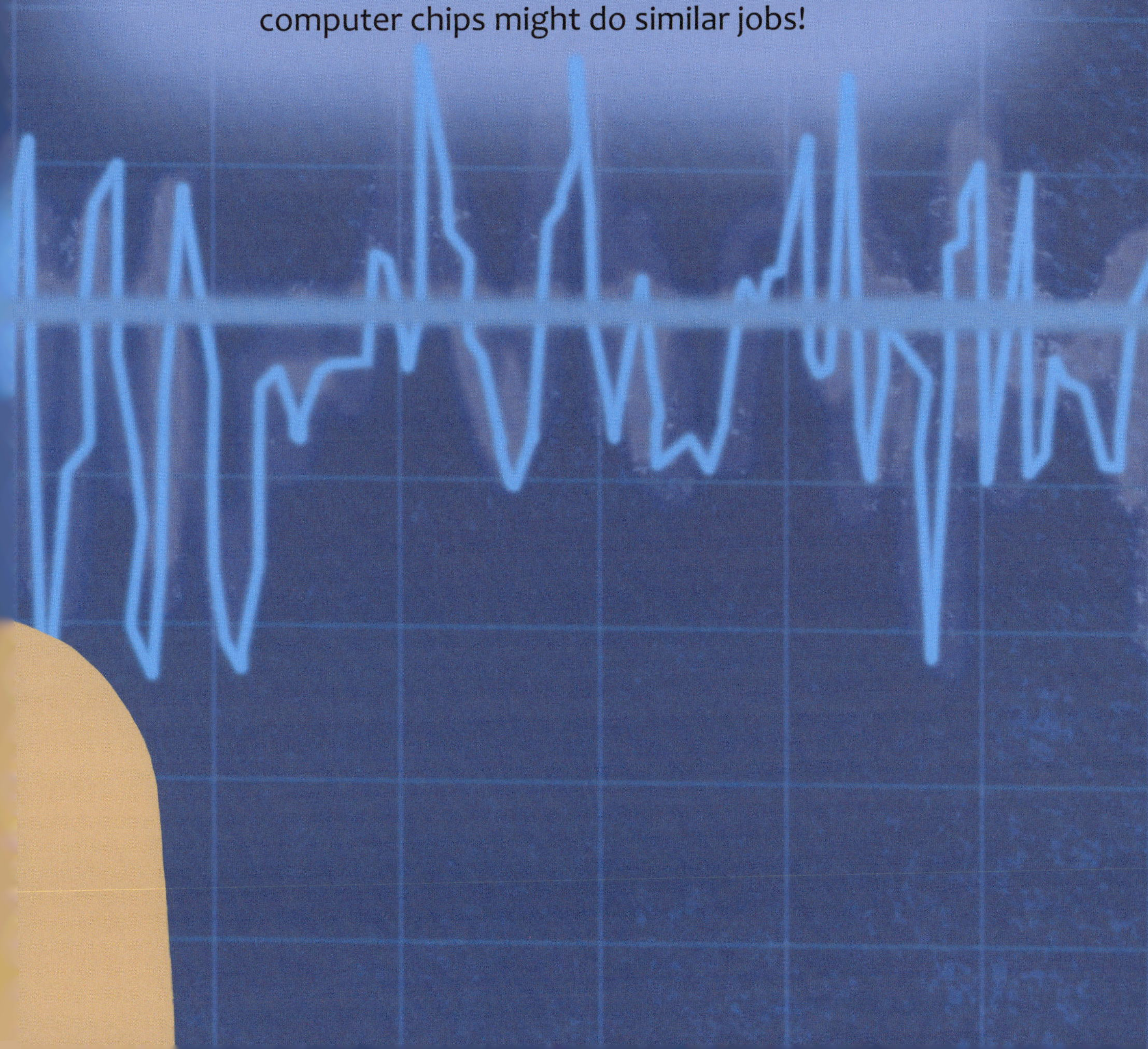

Technology is helping scientists do many things that once seemed impossible. They've even found a way for people to control robotic arms and legs **using only their minds!**

With help from **roboticists**, computers turn thoughts into real movements. This breakthrough could transform the lives of people who can't move or are missing limbs, giving them the ability to pick things up, run, and take part in sports!

What happens when the brain is pushed even further – like into outer space? It can change a lot!

In low **gravity**, liquids move differently within the body, increasing **pressure** inside the skull. This means some parts of **astronauts'** brains swell and others shrink – changes that can last for months! These discoveries could help teach us more about how the brain works.

Just like a computer, the brain needs lots of energy to keep working. It gets this energy from the air we breathe and sugar in the food we eat.

Scientists use powerful machines to scan the brain and measure the energy it needs to work. They've discovered that it uses about 20 **watts** of electricity, which is the same as a light bulb!

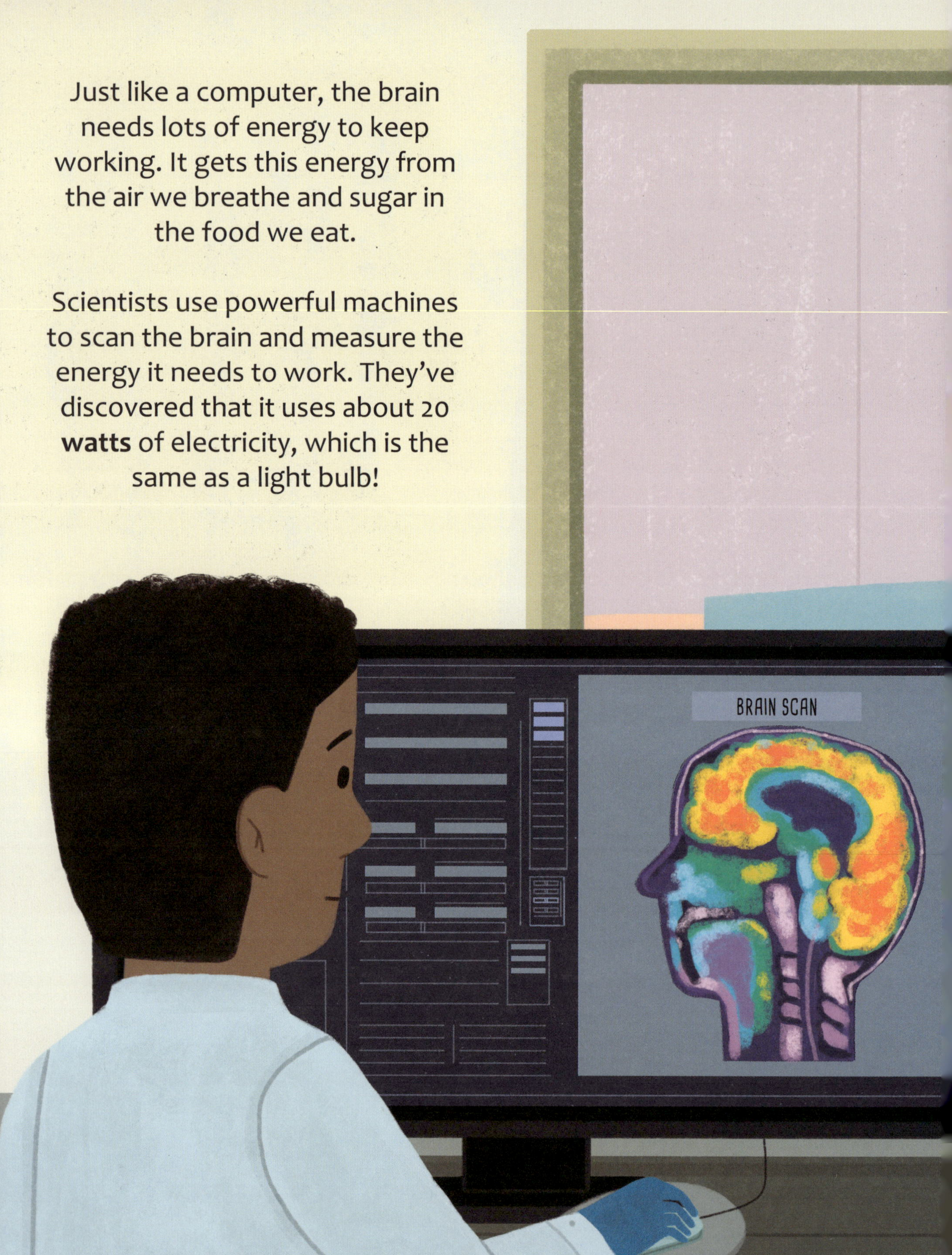

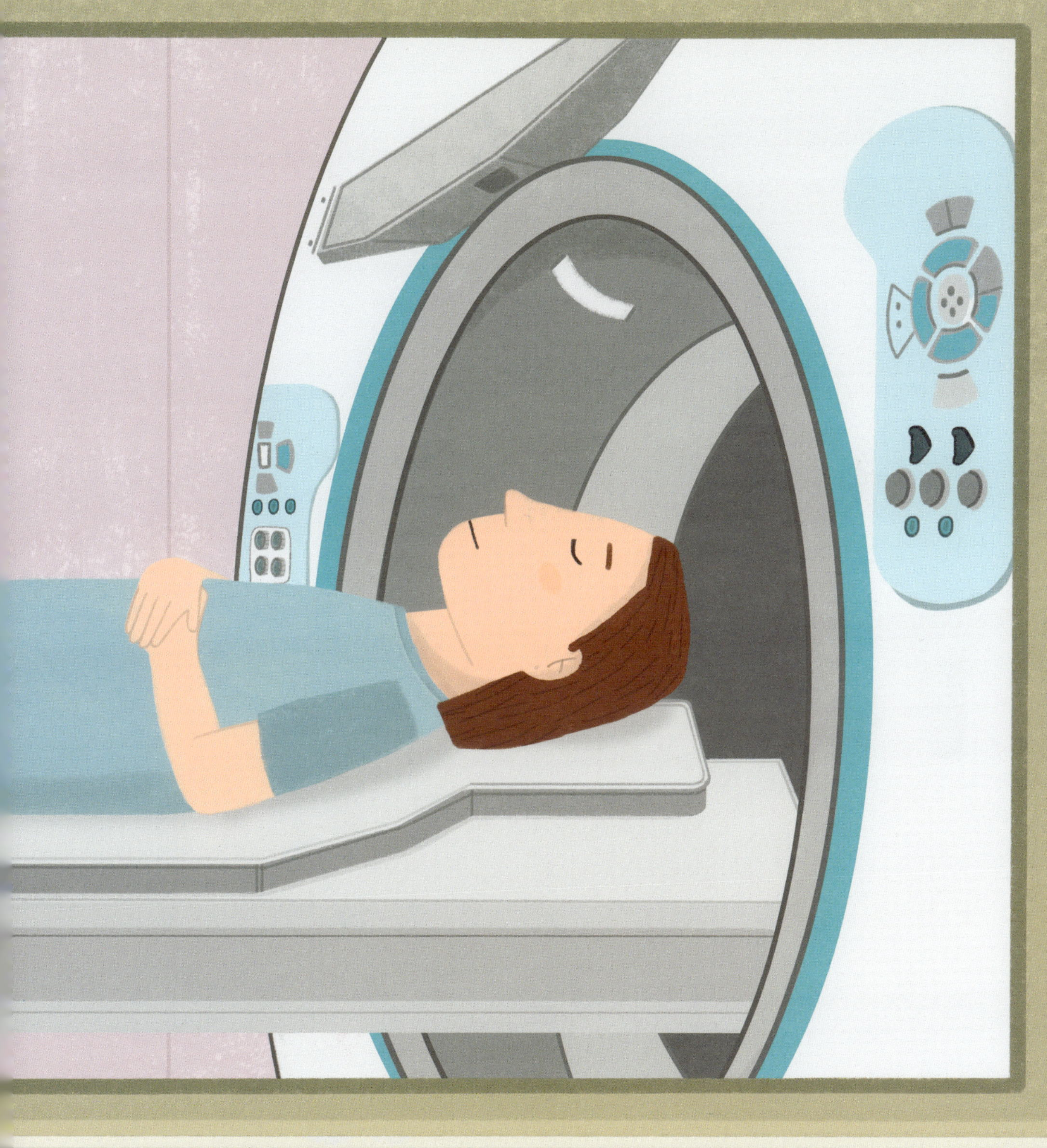

Because the human brain makes many short bursts of electricity, and light bulbs need a steady flow, we know the brain can't power a light bulb in real life. But if we could turn the bursts into a flow, it might just work!

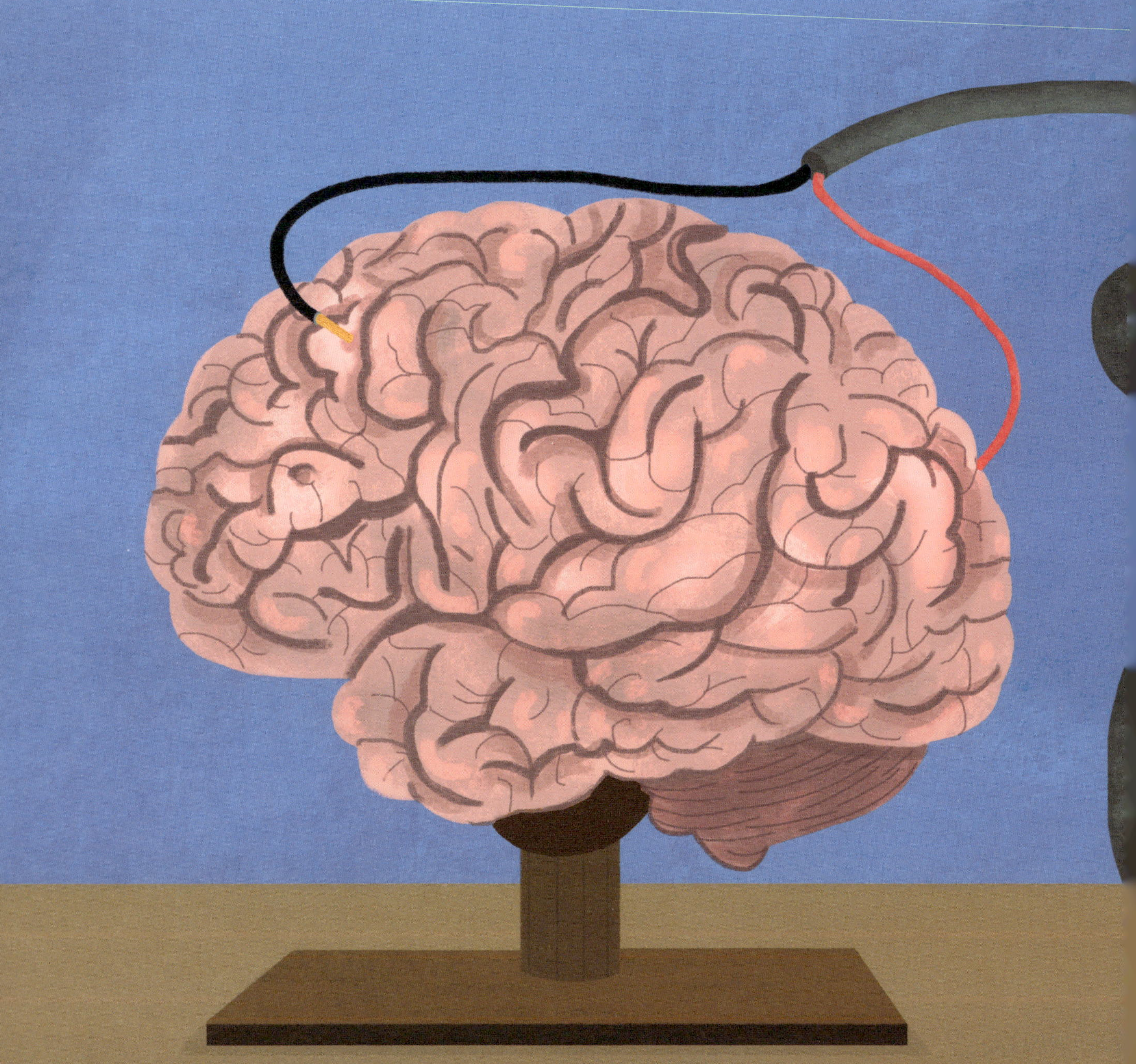

While the brain's electricity is impressive, thanks to clever scientists, we know its real power comes from what it lets us imagine, create, and feel.

Record-breaking

ANIMAL BRAINS

The human brain can do many incredible things, but it's not the only impressive brain in the animal kingdom. These animals all have record-breaking brains worth celebrating.

The biggest brain belongs to...

THE SPERM WHALE!

This ocean giant's brain is bigger and heavier than any other on Earth. It's more than five times the size of the human brain and weighs the same as a small dog!

The smallest brain belongs to...

THE NEMATODE WORM!

Nematode worms are so tiny they're hard to see without a microscope. Their brains are made of 302 neurons, making them the smallest brains of any **free-living** animal.

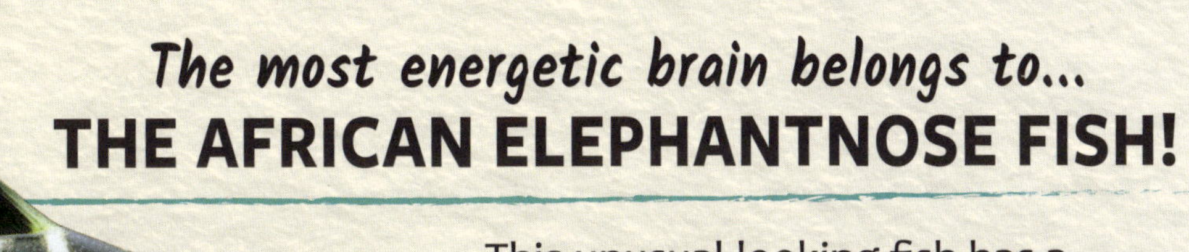

The most energetic brain belongs to...

THE AFRICAN ELEPHANTNOSE FISH!

This unusual-looking fish has a powerful brain. While it only takes up 3% of the size of its body, it uses more than 50% of the **oxygen** the fish takes in.

The largest brain for a small animal belongs to...

THE BRACHYMYRMEX ANT!

Also known as rover ants, *Brachymyrmex* have the largest brain for their body size. Their brains make up around 12% of their total body!

The biggest land animal brain belongs to...

THE AFRICAN ELEPHANT!

This huge, heavy brain holds billions of neurons, especially in the *cerebellum*. This area controls balance and coordination and helps the animal move its massive body.

Mind-blowing

BRAIN FACTS

There's so much to discover about the world of neurobiology. Did you know these fascinating facts about the human brain?

EVERYONE'S BRAIN IS UNIQUE!

Just like fingerprints, every person in the world has a **unique** brain. This is because our individual life experiences affect the shape of our brains and how they work.

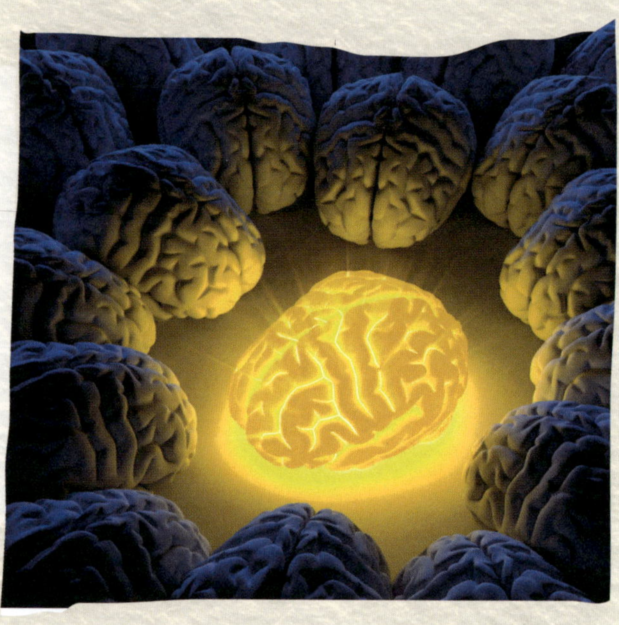

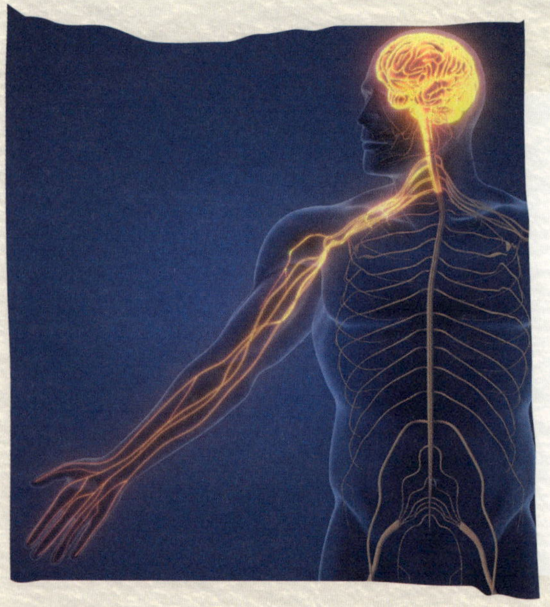

THE BRAIN FEELS NO PAIN!

The human brain doesn't feel pain, but it processes pain from other parts of the body. When you trap your finger in a door, **nerves** send a message to your brain and your brain tells your finger it hurts!

BRAIN SIZE DOESN'T MEAN EVERYTHING!

Scientists have debated whether animals with bigger brains are smarter than those with smaller brains. But most think brain shape and processing speed have more influence on intelligence than size.

THE HUMAN BRAIN NEEDS LOTS OF POWER!

Most human brains take up about 2% of the overall size of the body. But it takes about 20% of a human's energy to keep the brain working! That's a lot of power.

THE BRAIN LOVES WATER!

Scientists have discovered that the human brain is around 75% water. Not drinking enough water can affect our attention span, memory, and ability to make decisions.

GLOSSARY

Artifical – made by humans.

Astronauts – people trained to travel into outer space.

Disease – a condition that causes part of a living thing to no longer work properly.

Electrical currents – the flow of an electrical signal.

Free-living – an animal that isn't dependant on another for survival. A parasite isn't free-living.

Gravity – an invisible force that pulls things together. Gravity keeps your feet on the ground and keeps Earth spinning around the Sun.

Microscope – a scientific tool that makes small things look much bigger.

Nerves – thin, string-like parts of the body that carry messages between the brain and other body parts.

Nerve cells – also called neurons. Tiny parts of the body that send and receive messages to help you move and feel. Groups of nerve cells form a nerve (see left).

Nervous system – the network of body parts that control what you do and feel. It's made up of the brain, spinal cord, and nerves (see left).

Neurons – also called nerve cells (see above). *Need help saying this? Look below!*

Organ – a body part that's made of tissue (see right) and does a special job. The heart is an organ.

Oxygen – an invisible gas that plants produce, and people and animals need to breathe.

Parkinson's – a disease (see left) that affects the brain's ability to control the body's movements.

Pressure – the force of something pressing down on, or against, something else.

Roboticists – scientists who design and create robots.

Skull – the bony case that surrounds and protects the brain of a person or animal.

Spine – also called backbone. The line of bones down the middle of the back.

Tissue – a group of cells that perform a specific task inside the body, like muscles.

Unique – something that is one of its kind; unlike all others.

Watts – a unit of measurement that describes power.

HOW DO I SAY?

Brachymyrmex
BRACK-ih-mer-mex

Cerebellum
seh-reh-BELL-um

Nematode
neh-mah-TOAD

Neurobiologists
ny-ugh-row-by-OH-luh-jists

Neurobiology
ny-ugh-row-by-OH-luh-jee

Neurons
ny-UGH-rons

THE BIG QUESTIONS ANSWERED

This is more than just a series of books; it is a complete resource.
Accompanying each book is a variety of FREE material to engage curious kids with science.

www.thebigquestionsanswered.com

Use the QR code to visit the website, download free resources, and discover other books in the series.

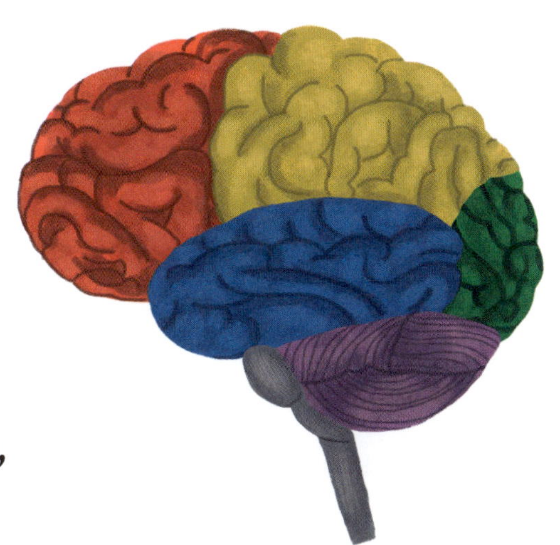

On the website, find out incredible things about neurobiologists, including what they do, some of their greatest discoveries, and the people who have made a difference in this field of science.

The material is also available for home or classroom use, supporting all the information in this book.

Teachers' & Parents' Resources
With discussion prompts, questions, and extra information around key topics.

Activity Pack
Fun activities including creative writing, word searches, and more.

Audio Book
Experience this book in audio, narrated by a professional voice actor.

The Big Questions Answered is published by Beetle Books.
Beetle Books is an imprint of Hungry Tomato Ltd.

First published in 2026 by Hungry Tomato Ltd
F15, Old Bakery Studios, Blewetts Wharf, Malpas Road,
Truro, Cornwall, TR1 1QH, UK.

ISBN 9781835691526

A CIP catalog record for this book is available from the British Library.

With thanks to:
Editors: Holly Thornton and Jenny Rowan
Designers: Meg Holbrook and Amy Harvey
The team at Beehive Illustration
Consultant: Dr Alexander Shaw

Information in this book is up to date as of the time of writing.

Printed and bound in China.

Picture Credits:
(t = top, b = bottom, m = middle, l = left, r = right)
Shutterstock: Anton Balazh 34mr; ArtLovePhoto 33mr; Boban_nz 33tl; DreamStudiopro 33bl; JitendraJadhav 34bl; Lightspring 35tl; Martin Prochazkacz 32ml; Tatiana Shepeleva 35bl; VLADFRIN 35mr.

Wikipedia: By Dan Dickinson, Goldstein lab, UNC Chapel Hill http://wormcas9hr.weebly.com/ - Own work, CC BY-SA 3.0, https://commons.wikimedia.org/w/index.php?curid=28800125 32bm.